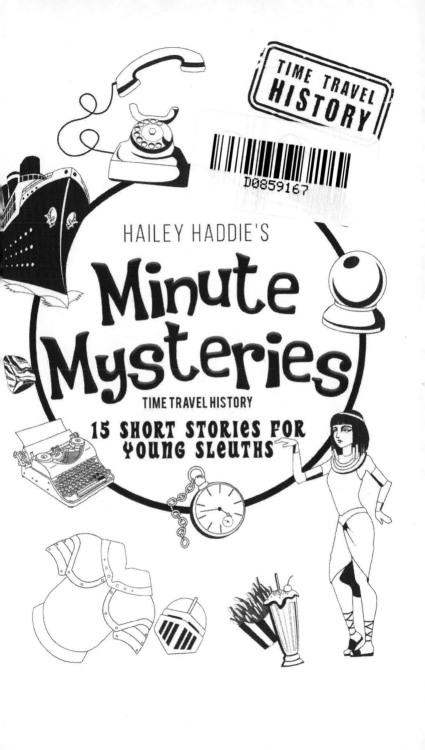

TIME TRAVEL
HISTORY

D0859167

HAILEY HADDIE'S

Minute
Mysteries

TIME TRAVEL HISTORY

15 SHORT STORIES FOR
YOUNG SLEUTHS

For aspiring amateur detectives with a knack for history— you have been challenged!

Written by Marina J. Bowman

Published by Code Pineapple

www.codepineapple.com

Contents

FOR DETECTIVE EYES ONLY:

From potion problems to royal ruses, I love to solve all mysteries! I may be known as the famous Hailey Haddie nowadays, but once I was just a young vampire detective with big dreams. Maybe you heard about me from junior crime solver Ellie "Scaredy Bat" Spark.

In the following pages, you will find a sampling of history-themed experiences taken from my case book. In these accounts, every clue necessary to the solution is given. The answer is in the story itself. You need look nowhere else.

These short stories can be read in about a minute and solved in a few more. The doodles that I have included may or may not be helpful for solving the mysteries. And some details in the story may lead to false conclusions.

I hope you will find them as enjoyable to read and solve as they were to record.

Good luck, detective!

—Hailey Haddie

Prologue

In a world filled with magic, mystical creatures, and other oddities, the time machine shouldn't have been such a strange sight. Maybe it was the tangle of wires and lights wrapped around it. Or possibly the thick stream of smoke billowing from the narrow chimney at the top. But I couldn't take my eyes off the coffin-turned-time-machine.

I couldn't believe that I had agreed to not only get into this smoking contraption, but to travel back in time to solve fifteen mysteries in a row. Even though Lou the inventor had explained many times, I still wasn't sure how he managed to erase the detectives of the past. However, I knew I could help. I could go back in time and solve their mysteries—or at least I hoped.

"I can do this. I'm Hailey Haddie, the great vampire detective," I whispered to myself, trying to boost my confidence. I gulped. The thought of time travel made my hands tremble.

A pungent gray puff of smoke wafted my way, clouding my thoughts and lungs. I coughed on the stench of burnt coffee and gasoline, but Lou didn't seem to notice.

Lou ran his tongue across one of his vampire fangs as he tightened a bolt on the malfunctioning time machine. With a few more turns and a kick, the machine lit up like a Christmas tree. Lou ran a greasy hand through his unruly hair, leaving behind a shiny black streak of grease. I nervously chewed the inside of my cheek.

"Alright Hailey, now get in!" he said. My feet felt like they were weighed down by bricks.

"You sure it's ready?" I asked. The machine sputtered and squealed, releasing a wisp of smoke.

Lou nodded. "As ready as it's going to be! We have to hurry. Without these cases solved, the whole future—our present—may never be the same. Until I can figure out how to bring the detectives back, I need you to go and solve their cases."

I gulped. "Fifteen mysteries in a row is a lot... What if I can't do it?"

"If anyone can do it, it's the greatest detective I know," Lou said with a wink. "I believe in you, Hailey!" He grabbed a tarnished bracelet and a pair of dangly sun earrings off a table piled with tools, scrap metal, and an apple on a blue plate. He dropped the jewelry in my hand. "Don't forget these."

"Jewelry?" I asked. I turned the sparkly orange earring and silver bracelet over.

"Not just any jewelry," Lou explained. "If you encounter other languages, the earrings will translate for you. They'll also disguise you as the original detective so you don't look out of place. And that bracelet, it will tell you where you are. Now put them on and get in the time machine." Lou opened the squeaky coffin door, and a loud *THUNK!* echoed from the machine.

My hands shook as I did what was instructed. As a vampire, I was used to coffins—after all, I slept in one every night. But this was different. The interior wasn't soft and welcoming like my cozy coffin bed outfitted with satiny blue sheets. Instead, the walls were worn and rickety, covered in pokey splintering wood.

"Remember, some mysteries will involve only humans. But others will take you into the past of the magic world," Lou explained. "You may find yourself in little-known places where magic was hidden in order to keep misunderstood magical beings and creatures safe. Good luck!"

With a loud beep and a hiss of frigid air, the door shut with a deafening click. The noisy machine and Lou disappeared, leaving me shaking in silent darkness.

"I can do this," I whispered to myself once more. "I'm Hailey Haddie, the great vampire—"

Before I could finish, a strong wind burst out of the floor and whooshed me into the air.

The Case of the

Lost Lapis Lazuli

In a puff of blue smoke, I appeared in a narrow hallway that smelled of wet earth, cinnamon, and myrrh. Colorful hieroglyphics adorned every inch of the rough, mud brick walls—paintings of pharaohs and Egyptian queens dancing were interspersed with flaming torches. Admiring the artwork illuminated by the soft flicker of flames, I almost forgot why I was there—until a piercing scream echoed throughout the palace. I, along with a pair of guards outfitted in billowy white skirts and striped headdresses, rushed into the room from which the cry came.

"What is wrong, my queen?" one of the guards asked. A woman with pin-straight, inky black hair, a blue stone necklace, and a long gold dress turned with her hands covering her eyes. Even without seeing her face, I knew immediately that she was the famous Cleopatra—the queen of Egypt.

"Go get Caesar!" she bellowed. The guards did as instructed, and the carved stone door shut with a heavy thunk. Like the hallway, the bedroom was illuminated by the glow of candles. It was sparsely furnished with a small wooden table in the corner beside a carved chest. They were the only furniture other than the bed on the opposite side of the room. However, the room felt far from bare thanks to the ornate cat paintings adorning the walls. The source of the art sat on a stool near the bed, hunched in the corner with a paintbrush in hand. He scratched his black beard before adding another glob of purple paint to a picture of a woman holding a kitten.

"What are you still doing here?" Cleopatra barked, peeking at me through a crack in her fingers.

I jumped. "I, um, I'm here to help," I answered.

After a moment of thought, she dropped her hands from her face, revealing her makeup-free eyes. There was no trace of her signature heavy eyeliner.

"My lapis lazuli is missing," Cleopatra explained.

To some that might have sounded like gibberish, but I knew of the stone thanks to my rock collection. My grandfather and I would often go hunting for different stones and gems down by the river and forest when I was growing up. It wasn't long before I had five shelves packed with rocks, including one with a few chunks of lapis lazuli. The vivid blue stone was hard to come by but had many uses—sleep potions, blue paint, a protection charm against evil, beadwork, and more.

"I am to meet Caesar and some advisors for dinner, and I cannot go without my blue eyeliner," Cleopatra added while re-covering her eyes.

"Can't you just pick another color?" I asked.

Cleopatra's red lips pulled into a frown as she peered at me through her fingers. "No! It is a special eyeliner that protects me from evil. And I refuse to leave here without it." She twirled on her heel and stormed to the other side of the room, signaling that our conversation had come to an end.

I started my investigation where her makeup lay on the wood table. A rainbow of powders was scattered across the grain, along with vials of animal fat. I sniffed one of the blubbery globs of fat and winced at the rancid scent. *It might be time to switch this out,* I thought to myself. I imagined the powders were mixed with the fat to create a paste, and never in my life was I so thankful for modern makeup.

Next, I inspected the painter's supplies. In his vials, he had every color—except for blue.

"No blue paint?" I asked.

He shook his head. "No. I haven't had blue paint in weeks." I picked up his orange paint to get a closer look. *Mix red + yellow paint* was scribbled on the label.

"You be careful with those!" he said. "I mixed them all fresh an hour ago." I agreed as I picked up the other vials.

White – mix chalk and gypsum

Red – mix iron and ocre

Purple – mix red + blue paint

Green – mix malachite

Yellow – mix arsenic trisulphide

I placed down the final vial just as Julius Caesar burst into the room.

"What is wrong, my love?" His muscular frame was draped in a white toga with a red stripe. My eyes wandered to the small blue stain near the bottom of the thin fabric.

"My lapis lazuli eyeshadow is missing!" Cleopatra explained.

"I will send all my men to find who stole it!" Caesar roared. "I won't sleep until it is in your possession again. I will—"

I cleared my throat. "I can save you the trouble—I know exactly where the lapis lazuli went."

Who took the lapis lazuli? How do you know?

HINT: THERE'S NO NEED to be blue.

SUPER HINT: Don't overthink it or you might get mixed up.

The solution is found on page 100

The Case of the

Saloon Secret

Sand makes for a soft landing when a time machine spits you out. But it gets absolutely everywhere. I shook the granules out of my cowboy boots and button-down as I headed to a group of buildings in the distance.

It was eerily quiet with not a soul in sight. The only sound in the old western town was the wind blowing. The dry desert sand danced in the wind, gingerly sprinkling a line of rickety wood shacks lining both sides of a sandy runway. As I made my way toward the one marked *Saloon*, multiple tumbleweeds blustered by.

Door chimes were followed by the creaks and moans of floorboards as I stepped into the abandoned establishment. A woman in a cowboy hat wiped the counter of a splintering wood bar. There were no seats lining it, but many tables with chairs scattered around. Most had dirty towels hanging nearby to use as napkins, and tarnished spit buckets were strewn throughout.

"We're closed," the woman muttered. "If you're looking for the gold mines, you've gone too far west."

"Oh um, I'm here—" I stepped forward, tripping on a stool. I regained my balance and found a pair of tired brown eyes staring at me.

"I said, we're closed," the woman repeated.

"I'm here to solve the mystery," I said.

The woman wrinkled her small button nose. "Mystery? You talkin' 'bout that robbery? I already told Joseph that I ain't talkin' to no sheriff or nothin'."

"I'm not a sheriff," I said. "But I can help."

The woman sighed. "Fine. Listen close. 'Cause I am only going through this once." I leaned against the bar and cleared my throat, trying to dispel the stale smoke that filled the establishment.

"I was working late, as always," she began. "About ten-fifteen at night, I go back to the safe in the office and I hear the door chimes. Well, I got a bad feeling since there have been lots of robbers 'round these parts lately. I turned out the lights in the office real quick, since there was a huge amount of money in the safe. I dialed the saloon owner, Joseph, and started to tell him what was going on, but the line disconnected. I then crept real quite-like to the open safe, gently shut the door, and crawled behind the big wood desk. Shortly afterward the robber entered my office, flashed his lantern over the place, and went to the safe. He had it open in a few minutes, took the money, and left. That's all I know about it."

"Do you happen to have the time?" I asked.

"I don't carry a watch," the woman said. "By the sun out there, though, it must be near five."

"How did you know it was ten-fifteen when you heard the door click?"

"That's easy," she said. "Joseph had some big date, so we closed early at ten. The break-in happened about twenty minutes after closing, I reckon. I forgot to lock the front door."

"You say the burglar was masked," I said. "How do you know that?"

The woman groaned. "Look, I'm not up for a million questions. I know he was masked because his lantern lit up his face when he cracked the safe."

"Can I see the office?" I asked.

"Fine, but be quick."

I followed her to the messy, windowless office. The smell of mold filled my nostrils as I walked into the damp room. The open safe sat empty near the desk littered with paper. A telephone with a curly cord and a rotary dial sat next to a stack of books. Unlike a cell phone, it had no lights, needed to be plugged into the wall, and was the size of a brick. I pointed to the device.

"Would you mind doing something for me?" I asked. "Can you call Joseph?"

She rolled her eyes. "If it will get you out of my hair sooner." She grabbed the phone, and, as I leaned against the wall, my elbow flicked off the light.

"Hey, what do you think you're doin'!" she yelled. "I can't see what number I'm dialing."

I switched the light back on. "Oops, sorry about that."

She scowled at me. "I ain't got time for this!" she spat, her eyebrows slamming together.

I gave a small smile. "Is that because you're too busy planning your next robbery? Your story isn't adding up."

What part of her story about the robbery didn't make sense?

HINT: You would need super vision to complete a task in the story.

SUPER HINT: Dial in on the details.

The solution is found on page 10

The Case of the

Diner Dash

In a flash, I landed on the grimy, black-and-white tiled floor of a diner bathroom.

"Oh, gross!" I cried, scurrying to my feet. I stepped to the sink and washed my hands, catching my reflection in the dirty mirror. I gasped. Not only had my clothing been changed to a formal brown suit, but my hair was short and slicked back. Plus, I had a mustache! After some of the shock wore off, I entered the diner.

Pablo Patsy, a famous singer from the fifties in the vampire world, crooned over the radio as waitresses in white dresses and rollerblades zipped around with trays full of food. The smell of greasy French fries and burgers made my mouth water. Food sizzled on the long grill behind the counter as cooks shuffled past one another, jumping from one task to the next. Posters advertising the specials hung above, curling from the heat of the grill.

1/4 pound burger, 48 cents.

Good Morning Breakfast Special, 30 cents.

Laughter squealed over the music. The source was a group of girls with pin curls, plaid shirts, and wool skirts at a table in the corner slurping milkshakes.

"Psst, over here," said a man with a crooked nose and acne scars sitting at one of the red leather banquet tables. I stared at him blankly. "What's wrong with you, Jeffers?" he asked, furrowing his brow. "It's me—Charles. Now take a seat."

I took a seat at the table with half-eaten food. There was a partial cup of coffee, broken ketchup bottle, pancake crumbs, and a plate full of salty

French fries. I automatically reached for a fry, but Charles slapped my hand away before I could snag one.

"What are you doing? Don't contaminate the crime scene!" he hissed. He looked around and lowered his voice. "We caught the man. He gave us quite the chase, though."

"Did he confess?" I asked, pulling my attention away from the food. I was utterly clueless what this man was talking about.

"Pfft, no way! But we got a witness," Charles said. He pointed to a blond waitress sitting at the counter. She was pale as a ghost with contrasting dark red lips. She took one of her trembling hands off her vanilla milkshake to rub her eyes. I had to resist the urge to gag—just the sight of vanilla milkshakes made me queasy. I once drank five in a row, which not only gave me the biggest stomach ache, but it made me never want to drink another one again. I pulled my attention back to Charles.

"The waitress said our suspect pulled out a stick that shot lightning, zapped the cashier, and made the girl vanish. A disappearing spell, I reckon, but I just spewed some story about how criminals got these new electric rods tech that can evaporate people. Almost made the blond waitress faint, but you know how people react around here with the mention of magic. They've only recently learned to accept vampires, and just barely."

I nodded, knowing how hard it was to have magic back in the 1950s. "So if you have a witness, then why am I here?" I asked.

Charles ran a hand through his slicked-back hair. "It ain't enough. We need proof, but this guy's good. He calmly ate at this table while planning the crime. He didn't give the girl a chance—just zapped her with his wand—and all for a few bucks. I tell you, detective, a man doesn't need much incentive to publicly use magic these days. After he cast his spell, he made a fast getaway in a waiting car."

"How was he caught then?" I asked.

"Fortunately, I was having dinner here at the time. I didn't see him zap her, but I'm the one that gave orders that nothing was to be disturbed at this table where the suspected criminal had eaten. There are zero fingerprints anywhere on the dishes or table here, but I think the suspect planned his attack while eating his dinner. However, we questioned the fool, and he claimed that he 'accidentally' cast that disappearing spell. And his attorney is confident that a jury will believe that."

I sat back and crossed my arms over my chest. "They shouldn't be so confident. There is a detail that proves he planned this."

What is the proof that the spell caster planned his attack?

HINT: THE SUSPECT TRIED to make a clean get-away.

SUPER HINT: Sometimes it isn't what you leave behind, but rather what you don't.

The solution is found on page 102

The Case of the
Gladiator Gambit

Swords clinked and clanked as I stumbled into the sweltering colosseum. Over fifty thousand cheering men and women sat or stood in the tiered benches skirting the fighting ring. Rich and poor cheered together—some draped in the finest jewels and clothing, while others wore mere rags that looked like they might disintegrate in the heat.

Men with metal helmets and breast plates swung the metal swords at each other in the dusty dirt. Their bare, muscular legs glistened in the sun, and I wondered why they didn't also have leg armor. If I was going to battle someone with a sword, I would definitely want leg armor!

"I think Spareveine is going to lose," said one kid holding a clay action figure that looked exactly like the gladiator fighting.

"Not a chance!" retorted the bald man. "Promegon will be victorious!"

Soon, the shorter gladiator took a swing at his opponent, hitting his chest and thrusting him to the ground. The hot, sweaty crowd erupted into more cheering. The winner joined the cries of glee as he lifted his sword in victory. "I defeated the mighty Promegon!"

While the crowd garnished the winner with their cheers, Promegon held my attention. He got back to his feet and slowly exited the fighting ring—but not before grabbing a piece of purple armor stuffed into a corner. My detective senses were telling me to follow him, so that's exactly what I did.

I tailed the man to a stone hallway, where he slipped on the scuffed, purple metal suit. Unlike his gladiator outfit, this one covered his body from head to toe. Only his eyes peeked out of the helmet. Once dressed, he led me around a set of marble statues depicting various fighters to a set of stairs with a door at the bottom. Two men stood in line before a guard at the door. As the men clad in colorful armor like Promegon passed through, the guard grabbed each of their wands to inspect them. Promegon held out the wand in his hand and turned it over.

"Flip it," the guard said in a gravely voice. Promegon abided. "Good luck," said the guard, waving him through.

"Stop," said the guard, holding out a large hand. My heart pounded like a jackhammer in my chest.

"Yes?" I gulped.

"Spectators are to use the entrance around the corner. This entrance is for fighters only."

I exhaled in relief. "Oh, okay. Sorry." I found the other door and entered an underground room that mirrored the colosseum above. While there weren't tiers of benches, there was a sandy fighting pit with one blue-armored gladiator ready to take the stage. Witches, wizards, and vampires lined the stands cheering. When I was a child, my grandfather told me stories about the magical fighting ring under the Greek colosseum, but I never imagined it was a real place. Sand showered down from the ceiling as patrons in the colosseum above erupted into a roar of cheers. This crowd soon did the same as Promegon joined the blue fighter and withdrew a wand from his armor.

A bony old man with matted hair and a red robe stood between them. He raised the hand of the blue fighter to introduce him.

"Delphinus!" he shouted in a surprisingly thunderous voice for such a small man. "Three-time champ and the best spell caster we've ever seen." The crowd cheered. The referee lifted Promegon's purple-armored hand next. "Promegon! He, um, has very nice purple armor!" He turned to Promegon. "Sorry, I asked around and no one seems to know much about you."

"I'm new here and just got in town last night for the fight, so no one knows me here," Promegon said.

The referee nodded and then held out both his hands. "Wands, please." The blue fighter willingly handed his over, but Promegon did not. He held his wand close to his chest, flipping it around.

"I'm sorry, but I don't let anyone touch my wand before a battle," he explained. "I believe it to be bad luck."

The referee handed the other wand back to the blue fighter. "Then let's just begin!"

The blue and purple armor clanked and clanged against shimmering yellow spells blasted from wands. It appeared much different from the fight I had witnessed earlier, but the crowd brought the same energy with hooting and hollering. Their boos shook the underground stadium as the old man wedged himself into the ring before the fight was over.

"There is a thief among us! This guard stole the golden wand!" He gestured toward the guard I had encountered earlier. Two other guards held his hands behind his back. "And he claims that Promegon is his accomplice. We do not allow criminals in this event."

The crowd gasped. "It's true!" spat the guard. "This was all his idea." All eyes fell on Promegon.

Promegon rolled his eyes. "That's a lie! I've only seen this man once before in my life, and it was when he let me in a few moments ago."

I ran into the middle of the ring.

"No, *that's* a lie!" I shouted. "I have a strong suspicion these men knew each other before."

What evidence shows that Promegon and the guard knew each other before their door interaction?

HINT: CRIME CAN BE a touchy subject.

SUPER HINT: Superstition leads to a super clue.

The solution is found on page 103

The Case of the

Royal Ruse

Queen Eleanor's flowy fabric headdress topped with a gold crown was exactly how the history books depicted her. Her pale skin glowed in the morning light as she looked me over in the castle's throne room. Finally, she threw back her long red hair and took a seat on her throne. My eyes trailed over the spotless tile floor in the room. There wasn't a speck of dust in sight.

A woman with large blue eyes and black hair came through the door balancing a tray of fruit. Eleanor instantly shooed her away. "Thank you, Marie. But I can't possibly think of food when my beloved husband, King Henry II, is dying from a mysterious poisoning."

"Sorry, my queen," the girl mumbled while making a quick exit. Once again, we were alone. "What happened to Louis?" I asked, assuming that was why I had been sent there.

"My husband left for dinner without me last night. I stayed behind to wait for my new shoes to arrive and then was to join him." The queen looked down at her shoes lovingly. "Well, soon after Marie finally delivered my shoes, just as I was ready to leave, I heard screams. News traveled to me that my beloved had been poisoned!"

"Do they have any idea who did it?" I asked.

The queen shook her head. "No, but my husband has been known to make enemies. They suspect someone slipped poison in his drink. How am I ever supposed to eat or drink anything again? How am I ever supposed to leave this room? I've been here since yesterday morning because I'm too afraid that the same person will try to attack me if I leave."

I walked to the corner, where dirty rags sat in a neat pile. "What are these?" I asked.

The queen ignored my question, analyzing her shoes, which were poking out from her long skirt. She bent over to rub a muddy spot on one.

"Marie! Marie!" she hollered. "There is already mud on my new shoes."

The same servant girl as before rushed in with a new pair of shoes and took the muddy ones. As Marie exited, she tripped, dropping the shoes. A small vial rolled out of her dress and onto the floor. She managed to snatch it back up before the queen noticed.

Marie ran out without looking back at the queen or me. When the door shut, Queen Eleanor turned her attention back to me.

"So what are you going to do about this? Do you know who did this?"

"I have my suspicions," I answered.

Who is the primary suspect and why?

HINT: SOMEONE IS KEEPING a dirty little secret

SUPER HINT: If the shoe fits...

The solution is found on page 104

The Case of the

Cave Conundrum

In a flash and cloud of smoke, I fell to the pebbly floor of a dimly lit cave. The stale, damp air filled my lungs as I got to my feet. I approached a hysterical crowd of cave people, the wet rocks feeling slimy under my bare toes.

"We'll get you out!" a woman with unkempt hair yelled frantically at a rock wall. The baby in her arms wailed, intermingling with the panicked voices throughout the area. Cave men and women with torches grunted as they pushed and pulled at the rock walls covered with paintings. The basic drawings depicted men hunting rabbits, women gathering fruit, and woolly mammoths with tusks like elephants. They were all in brown, red, and black,

36

except for the rabbits. The rabbits were painted in gold.

"What's happening?" I asked a man with a brow covered in filth.

"She's stuck! Once you get in, you can't get out," he said, beating the wall with a wooden club. A painting of flowers crumbled slightly under the club's force. A few more hits and the beating stick snapped.

"Argh!" the man yelled, throwing the club. The splintered wood landed by a foot-wide crack on the other side of the cave that ran from the ceiling to the floor. I grabbed a fiery torch to investigate. Sucking in my stomach, I slipped through, and, right before my eyes, the crack healed over. I pushed where the opening once was, but it was now solid rock.

I gulped. With only one way to go, I followed the narrow drippy passage, stopping at a pile of axes and weapons fashioned from sticks and carved stones.

I reached down and picked up a bone carved like a snake. I always said if I couldn't be a detective, I would be a sculptor. And I recognized this sculptural carving from a library book I once read. This tribe was part of an early civilization that lived in caves, living off the land by hunting and gathering. They would feast off of woolly mammoth, deer, and other creatures, but no animal was more prized than the rabbit. With their speed and jumping ability, they were a difficult catch. So when a tribe caught a rabbit, they would throw a celebration around the fire as it cooked.

I continued through the leaky passage until I reached a small room. Much like the cave, the walls were plastered in drawings. Mountain lions bathing by a pond, rabbits leaping through fields, and snakes slithering up trees. The only wall that didn't have any drawing held a heavy stone door covered in glittering gems. Carved in the rock wall beside it were the words: *Keep your eye on the treasure if you want to leave.*

"Hello?" whispered a small voice from a dim corner. A scrawny girl covered in dirt emerged from the darkness. Her bony hand grasped a rag that looked like a well-loved blanket.

"Are you the one who's stuck?" I asked.

"Yes," she said with a trembling lip. "Momma told me not to go in here, but I didn't listen. Once you're in, you can never leave. It doesn't matter how hard you push or pull that door. It never opens."

"I don't think you have to push or pull to open that door," I said. "It looks magic." Sure enough, I was right. We followed the door's instructions and were able to leave. The girl's family was very thankful I rescued her and offered to have a rabbit feast in my honor.

How did we get through the door?

HINT: ALL THAT GLITTERS isn't gold.

SUPER HINT: One man's food is another man's treasure.

The solution is found on page 105

The Case of the
Potion Problem

The metal shelves in the stuffy storage closet rattled and shook as I fell to the cold tile floor with a hard crash.

"I guess time machines don't spit you out gently," I mumbled. I got to my feet and stumbled forward, knocking a shelf. A rainbow orb rolled off a second shelf and smashed to the floor in a burst of colorful glitter and glass shards. My feet wobbled in black heels—which I definitely wasn't wearing when I entered the time machine. My casual pants and shirt had also transformed into a black dress. I sighed, hoping that breaking a rare orb didn't affect the future or anything.

I stepped around a shelf holding wands and vials of sparkling liquid to reach the door. As soon as I stepped through, I was blinded by the morning sunlight blazing through the windowed wall. I stood frozen in the corner of the hot, bustling room where plants and flowers bloomed throughout. A line of cauldrons ran straight through the middle, each with a tired-looking witch stationed in front of it. Their outfit wasn't the only thing the same about all of them—they all also sported gaunt cheeks and heavy bags under their eyes. Black heels dragged all around me as the workers hurried about to gather ingredients for their brews. While the witches seemed lethargic, their concoctions energetically sizzled and flamed.

"Excuse me," said one short redhead with an angular face. She pushed past me into the closet I had just come from and emerged with a box of snails. "Careful in there!" she warned. "Someone broke some glass." She scurried off to her cauldron in the far corner before I could say anything.

What on earth am I supposed to do here? I thought. I recognized the place as *Potions Express*, a failed business that "hired" witches to make potions in bulk. Many traditional witches were against the idea of commercializing potions, and eventually the building burnt down in a protest. A law passed soon after making it illegal to create and sell potions in bulk after the company was found to have blackmailed many witches into working for them. Practicing witches could either work there, or the company would reveal to the world that they were witches, making the women vulnerable to exile—or worse.

As I wobbled forward on my heels, a woman with dark curly hair raced out of an adjoining room.

"Someone stole the dragon's breath!" she cried. The clinking and clanging of potion-making stopped, and the witches collectively gasped. Whispering broke out as the curly-haired woman fainted and slumped to the ground.

Instinctively, I rushed into the room from which she had come. It was a black and white office that looked like a tornado had struck it. Books scattered the starry tiled floor, along with broken candlesticks and shattered vials of liquids. The glass shards crunched under my heels as I stepped over a fallen four-tier shelf toward a golden safe on the wall. It was open and empty. As I walked to the other side of the room, my foot hit a rainbow orb. It rolled into the corner, where a silver statue of an oak tree stood as high as the ceiling. I picked up the colorful ball and placed it on the orderly desk. Multiple other rainbow orbs were sitting on the floor, but I didn't have time to rescue them—the curly-haired woman had awoken.

"Last night, someone snuck in while I was working late," she explained. "I couldn't see them because it was dark, but they cast a sleeping spell on me. The last thing I remember is seeing the shelf being shoved to the ground. The code to the safe was hidden in a book there, so they must have found it, opened it, and taken all the dragon's breath."

"Was there anything else important on the shelf?" I asked.

The woman shook her head. "Not really. There were a few rainbow orbs on the top shelf, but they all seem to be here. The thief only wanted the dragon's breath."

"Why didn't you report this when you woke up?" I asked.

"I just woke up before I passed out in the main room," she said. "I'm going to call the police right now."

"Unless you also plan on turning yourself in, I wouldn't do that. Your story doesn't add up."

Why doesn't the curly-haired woman's story add up?

HINT: HAVE AN IDEA? Just roll with it.

SUPER HINT: You have to be on the ball to solve this one.

The solution is found on page 106

The Case of the

Salem Scandal

An old woman with crooked, yellowing teeth leaned against a wooden cane. Her stiff dress puffed out at the hips and grazed the yellowing grass. It was complete with a gold belt, a lace neck frill, and sleeve ruffles.

A bird zipped past the limestone colonial house behind her and perched itself onto the red clay roof. A bundle of frizzy gray hair escaped from underneath her wired lace headdress as she lifted her head to sneer at the chirpy creature. "Shoo!" she yelled. "Shoo!" Satisfied once the bird flew off toward the nearby lake, she turned her attention to a young girl with blond hair and fair skin.

"Amira used her witchcraft to steal the gold!" she sneered. She lifted her cane and pointed to the trembling girl. "I should turn you in, so they can get rid of you like those other witches."

"I swear, I didn't steal anything," Amira said. She looked at me with big, pleading eyes. "You have to believe me, detective."

"Well, someone had the nerve to commit such a robbery at high noon," mused Professor Gramford. "The gold was gone from the hiding spot!" His long petticoat and ruffled shirt danced in the wind as he scratched one of his legs, clad in tight pants. "Same old story: no fingerprints, no evidence."

The old woman shooed Amira away, ordering her to start preparing lunch. Amira disappeared inside.

"Is it just the three of you that live in this house?" I asked.

"No. John, my nephew, is also staying here for the summer," Professor Gramford answered. "Why don't you come inside?"

I stepped inside the entryway of the house. A small fire burning in the stone fireplace on the other side of the sparsely furnished room gave the air a woodsy scent.

I examined a sheet of ripped parchment on the nearby desk. It looked like a half-written note regarding witches living in Salem.

"Where is John now?" I asked.

"Oh, he left about an hour ago to do some fishing," the professor answered.

A few minutes later, I noticed Jones, the gardener, working at the edge of a flowerbed. He kept glancing at the house while he frantically covered over the hole he had dug. Finishing, he hurriedly walked toward the dock.

I followed, reaching the dock just as John guided his wooden paddle boat in.

"Have a nice day?" I asked.

"Sure did," John answered. "Caught some good fish!"

I helped the men tie up the boat and then continued my questioning. "Where were you when your uncle's gold was robbed today?"

"I was hauling in a big muskie! What a battle he gave me! See him at the end of the boat? Isn't he the biggest fish you ever laid your eyes on?"

I turned my attention to the gardener. "And where were you today?"

"I was, uh, I headed to town to run an errand," he replied nervously, glancing at John.

"That's very vague," I said. "When did you get back from this 'errand'?"

"It was about noon," the gardener answered reluctantly before taking off toward the house.

"John, do you know where your uncle stashed his gold?" I inquired.

"Is that old weasel accusing me?" John huffed. "Him and that old bat are just mad because I've taken a liking to Amira, their housekeeper."

"No, he isn't. But I have a suspect in mind."

Who is the suspect? Why?

HINT: Timing is everything.

SUPER HINT: When I was fishing for information, someone knew something that logically couldn't have been known.

The solution is found on page 107

The Case of the

Petrified Passenger

I was on the biggest ship in history, and I also had one of the biggest stomachaches. Not even the crisp, cool night air could calm my seasickness. The tall smoke stacks poking out of the ship let off another puff of smoke as my stomach churned.

I tried to turn my attention to the starry sky, but looking up just made me queasier. While I loved swimming and snorkeling, something about being on a boat always made me seasick. All I could think of was my friend Aria's tenth birthday party. Her parents had rented a sailboat to take us all out on the ocean. I ended up tossing my cookies just before they cut the cake—ruining everyone's appetite. My stomach lurched as a gust of wind brushed past me.

Then, just as I thought I was going to relive the sailboat incident, a woman burst through a nearby door.

"Come quick, detective!" she bellowed breathlessly. "There's a man in the cabin next to me. It looks like he has petrified himself. He is as frozen as a statue, and twice as cold as an iceberg!" The woman was easy to follow, since her poofy pink dress with a corset was hard to lose sight of. I chased her inside toward a grand double staircase with a thick, carved wood railing. A statue of a person holding a torch sat in the middle, casting extra light over the extravagant carvings on the rails and wood walls. Centered on top of the stars on the ceiling was a frosted glass dome. I imagined during the day that sunlight bathed the area in a dreamy glow.

The curved stairs led us into a carpeted hallway lined with doors on either side. Four doors down, we entered the room on the right. I stepped into a large cabin where a woman in a yellow dress sat sobbing beside the victim. A man dressed in a jacket was lying face down with a wand clutched in his left hand.

I stepped over shards of clear glass as I inspected the room. The single bed tucked into the corner was made without a crease, the velvety green sheets perfectly in place. I admired the strips of gold that accented the creamy white walls with inlays on golden brown wallpaper on some of the panels. Nearby was a round table with four armless wooden chairs tucked in. A golden lamp was perched in the middle. I flicked its switch, but it wasn't plugged in. Nearby I found luggage and a right-hand leather glove, turned inside-out.

"Does this glove belong to the victim?" I asked. "What about that soiled handkerchief on the table?" Both women shrugged.

"We just heard a noise and rushed over. We're staying in the next room," explained the one in the pink dress. I turned over the body and unbuttoned the topcoat. The girls gasped.

"That's Jeffrey Brenburg, the millionaire!" the yellow-dress girl cried. The body was immaculately clothed in the finest custom tailoring.

"Looks like he broke his pocket watch, too. Stopped at eight-ten," I observed as I removed the timepiece from the vest pocket. It was missing the glass face. "Let's see if those pieces of glass on the floor are part of the watch." Sure enough, they were. I turned my attention back to the lone glove. "One thing that bothers me is that single glove," I said. "Where is the other?"

"We can help look," said the pink-dress girl. The three of us searched the room but found no trace of the other glove.

As our search concluded, I turned to both women. "Thank you for all your help. While this does look like a statue spell was cast on Jeffrey, I don't believe he did it to himself."

What made me suspect someone else cast the statue spell on the victim?

HINT: PIECING THIS ONE together is hard.

SUPER HINT: What would be impossible if the victim fell facedown?

The solution is found on page 108

The solution is found on page 108

The Case of the

Blueprint Burglary

The inventor of the microwave, Percy LeBaron Spencer, sat in the rickety wooden chair in the corner of his small office. Beside him was a stack of books with a rotary phone precariously perched on top. The room held the scent of burnt-out candles and despair. I paced the room as he told me the story of the theft. I got dizzy from going back and forth so much, since his office was only five steps long.

"I was sitting right here when a man with a bat entered the room and stood motionless for a few seconds," said Percy, cleaning his black-rimmed glasses. "Apparently satisfied no one was here, he walked to the desk over there in the corner. As he rummaged through the papers in the drawer, I hastily dialed headquarters, but no one answered."

"You say he took nothing but the blueprints for Methods of Treating Foodstuffs from your desk?" I asked, looking over an oak desk jammed against one wall. Heaps of papers sat in metal baskets beside a typewriter and a stack of yellowing newspapers.

"He may have also stolen blueprints for something else, but I can't be sure," Percy answered. His eyes trailed to the dusty green-and-burgundy carpet under his shiny dress shoes. "I really need to clean this place up sometime."

"Rather careless to leave such an important paper lying about like that, wasn't it?" I asked.

Percy rubbed the bridge of his nose. "I know, it really was. But it was only a copy. I sold the original yesterday."

"Would that blueprint be valuable to anyone else?" I asked.

"Yes, it would be worth twice as much to my buyer's competitors. Would you like some tea?" Percy asked. "I believe I have some of those new square tea bags. Such an odd shape, but the tea is good!"

"No, thank you," I said. "Why didn't you sell it to them in the first place, then?" I asked, turning the conversation back to the investigation.

"My buyer financed me while I was perfecting the patent, so I thought it only right to sell it to him, even though I could have got more for it from the other firm. Silly move on my part."

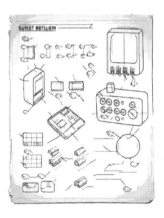

The pale skin on Percy's face had begun to flake, revealing green scales underneath. Ignoring the physical anomaly, I continued. "As this is such a small, bright room, you should be able to give me a *very* good description of the intruder."

"Oh, I can do that," Percy replied, with assurance. "He was a big fellow, about six feet tall, and weighed around two hundred pounds. He had jet-black hair, an unusually large nose, and a vicious-looking mouth. As he left obviously unaware of my presence, I noticed he had a big rip in the back of his blue coat."

"Well, Percy, I don't think there is much I can do," I said, leaning against the corner desk.

Percy shot up from his chair, more of his skin flaking. "What do you mean? Can't you go question my buyer? Maybe he knows something and can help."

"Well, for one, you're clearly a shapeshifting elf and not really Percy LeBaron Spencer." I pointed to his crusty skin. "Your face is falling off. BUT, putting your skin issues aside, the story you spun is unbelievable and can't possibly be true."

What part of the shapeshifting elf's story couldn't be true?

HINT: SOMETIMES IT'S THE small things that help crack the case.

SUPER HINT: The robber wasn't blind or deaf.

The solution is found on page 109

The Case of the

Reptile Riddle

The smell of roast chicken and crab cakes wafted through the air of the grand dining room. A long table that required two crystal chandeliers to illuminate it held a mix of men and women in their best party clothes. Women in polka-dot party dresses and men in finely pressed suits laughed and chatted as they drank and snacked on appetizers. I was so busy taking in the flower wallpaper lined with oversized oil portraits of dogs that I didn't notice a man with a monocle and thick black mustache approach the record player behind me. He lifted the needle off the spinning black disc, bringing the soft instrumental music to a stop. There was something comforting and familiar about him, but I couldn't put my finger on it.

"We are all ready to take a seat now. And as per tradition, we're ready for you to read the dinner party mystery." His vampire fangs gleamed as he gave me a toothy smile.

"Dinner party mystery?" I asked.

He pointed to the stack of parchment with scribbled handwriting at the end of the table. Then, he took a seat beside me. The room quieted, and everyone else followed. All twenty-four pairs of eyes were on me.

I cleared my throat as I picked up the papers. They shook in my hand as I stuttered out the first words.

'Tom had a big party last night,' said Grant, the valet.

'Certainly looks like it,' retorted the detective. He surveyed the crazily balanced glasses on the white table, the tables ruined with water rings, and a mysterious blue stain on a plush white carpet. The butler stood in the corner by a broken bookcase.

'It was awful, detective,' said the butler. 'Just as I turned to say "good night" to him, he lifted his wand and turned himself into a lizard. He must not have done it right, though. Just as he was passing that white table over there, he turned back into a human. He fell down on it with a hard crash and has been passed out there ever since.'

'Was anything bothering Tom?' inquired the detective.

'Vera, his former wife, was here last night. He always acts weird after seeing her. He doesn't miss her or anything, but she took the cat, Fluffums, when they split. He loved that cat!'

'Has anything been touched since the tragedy?' asked the detective.

'No, sir.'

The detective picked up Tom's wand from where it had apparently fallen from his hand. After examining it and finding only Tom's fingerprints, he laid it on the table beside the wobbly tower of glasses. As he did so, Vera entered the room. She stopped, horrified.

'What—what—has happened?' she cried.

'Where did you come from?' demanded the detective.

'I've been upstairs. I didn't leave with the guests.'

'Humph—you should have,' said Grant as he shot her a quizzical look. 'Your presence is mighty fishy.'

'That's not the only thing fishy about this mystery,' said the detective. 'Someone is lying.'

What is fishy about this situation? How does the detective know someone is lying?

I put down the paper just in time to see the monocled man beside me lean back in his chair.

"Ah, this is a tough one," he said.

"It is not!" came a woman's voice from the far side of the table. The monocled man couldn't take his eyes off the brown-haired beauty in the black polka-dot dress as she explained what didn't fit in the situation.

"That is quite genius, Gertrude," said the man.

My jaw dropped. I knew why the man was familiar—he was my grandfather! And the smart woman that solved the mystery? My grandmother, Gertrude. Her skin may have been smoother, and her hair was brown instead of gray, but her large blue eyes still held the same twinkle. He always said that he fell in love with her the moment she showed off her big brain at a dinner party.

I grinned as my grandmother pulled up a chair closer to my grandfather. Crazy to think that if they had never met and fallen in love, I might have never been born.

What was fishy about the story I read aloud for the dinner party mystery?

HINT: DETECTIVE WORK IS sometimes a balancing act.

SUPER HINT: Tom shouldn't have been the only thing that fell.

The solution is found on page 110

The Case of the

Inheritance Intrigue

The polished wooden floorboards creaked under my flats with each step. A group of boys in blazers and tweed pants smiled and nodded to me as they quietly passed to reach the back of the library. I was so awestruck by my surroundings that I almost forgot to smile back.

Every wall in the open room with twelve-foot ceilings was covered in books. The domed stained-glass ceiling poured a rainbow over the shelves of endless reads. I ran my fingers over the gold-embossed book spines, wishing I had time to read just one. They had a wonderful new paper smell that made my heart leap with joy. I wandered a little farther to the side of the long room that held round tables fitted with gold banker's lamps. A cluster of girls with pin curls and dresses studied books and scribbled notes in one corner. And in the other corner sat a girl with dishevelled short brown hair, a long wool skirt and button down sweater. Worry lines nipped at the corners of her eyes as she fiddled with her pearl necklace. Something told me she was why I was here.

The creaky floor played its signature tune as I approached her. As I got closer, I noticed she also wore dark red lipstick. Her ink-stained hand grasped a silver pen that scribbled on a sheet. She paused, held up the sheet, crumpled it, and threw it to the ground.

"Gah!" she cried.

"Shh!" said the group of girls in unison.

The writer slumped in her seat. "Sorry," she whispered, before writing on a fresh sheet. With no mystery in sight, I picked up the crumpled sheet nearby. My heart stopped when I saw the name scribbled at the top of the page—Agatha Christie. My all-time favorite mystery author! When I was growing up, I used to stay awake all night with a flashlight under the covers to finish her novels. And now, I got to read something she hand-wrote. Possibly something no one else had ever seen. With a shaky hand, I read the crumpled paper.

"The tranquil countryside melted into the darkness as the car pulled away. Jim Schlepper, the brother of New York's largest theatrical producer, waved good-bye to his family standing outside by the towering white mansion. He would miss them dearly, but was glad to be travelling again.

He arrived in Europe a week later, registering at Hôtel Chat. At two o'clock next morning, he called the office and demanded he be given another suite immediately, saying he didn't like the grouchy orange cat that lived there. This was odd, considering Mr. Schlepper had occupied—in fact, insisted upon—this suite many times in the past. Because of his prominence and wealth, he was accommodated at once, giv-

en the ever-popular suite that was home to a fluffy gray cat named Pewter.

Moving on to Berlin four days later, he registered at the Hotel Katze. The manager, anxious to please a brother of the internationally known producer, greeted him personally. He afterward remarked how worried Mr. Schlepper appeared at the time.

At two o'clock in the morning, a repetition of the Paris occurrence took place—Mr. Schlepper demanded a new suite.

From Berlin he went in turn to London, Copenhagen, Brussels, Vienna, Bucharest, and Sofia, spending exactly four days in each place. He then went to Persia. He explained to a friend over dinner that he had come to Persia for two reasons. One: to find the *finest cat. Two: to continue his search for one Miss Minarah, a mystic he had met in New York, and for whom he had sought vainly all over Europe.*

On the fourth day in Persia, Mr. Schlepper was found in his hotel room—petrified and turned to rock. The authorities couldn't reverse the rare witch's spell in time.

Receiving news of his death, his attorney in New York opened Mr. Schlepper's will. It was found that he had left his entire fortune of two million dollars to the famous producer.

But, strange as it may seem, it was found that Mr. Schlepper never had a brother. What a situation!

If the man had no brother, whom did his inheritance go to?"

Agatha Christie snatched the crumpled sheet just as I finished. "Oh my, don't read that!" she squealed. "It's absolutely horrid. I just can't seem to write anything good lately." With a sigh, she tossed the paper on a stack of other sheets perched on the desk's corner.

I gulped, knowing exactly what this moment in history was. In her biography, Agatha said she was ready to give up on writing mysteries after a series of rejections. That is, until a mysterious woman in the library complimented her work, giving her the confidence boost she needed to continue. Her work would be published a year later in 1920.

"I did read it. And I actually thought it was quite clever," I assured Agatha, trying to keep my voice steady. "You seem to have quite the knack for writing mysteries."

A small smile curled at her lips. "Really!? Were you able to figure out the mystery?"

I nodded. "It took me a second, but I figured it out."

If the man had no brother, who did his inheritance go to?

HINT: THE INHERITANCE WASN'T meant for any man.

SUPER HINT: Siblings come in many shapes and sizes.

The solution is found on page 111

The Case of the

Camelot Curse

BRITAIN, LATE 5TH CENTURY

My clothes were dripping in water and mud as I walked toward the gray castle. Rounded columns shot up on each side with soggy flags hanging limply in the rain. The drawbridge lowered, and two knights in armor led me through mud and rain to the front door. The downpour made a light tinging sound as it sprinkled their heavy metal plates.

I removed my shoes in the spotless entryway and was led through a room that held a large, round table into a small living room. A bright fire crackled in the fireplace, illuminating a man with a graying beard and gold crown snoring on a clean, white fur carpet.

"We've tried to wake King Arthur," said a butler, sitting behind a woman with a gold crown. "But we can't. Can you figure out what happened and fix it?" I told him I would try my best and approached the snoring king.

My attention was attracted to a gold coin about five feet from the sleeper. I picked up the coin with the silver star on it and regarded it curiously. I knew of only one species that carried a coin of that type—vampires. It was a good luck charm that was used to ward off evil.

"What did you find?" asked the butler, cocking an eyebrow.

"Not much, yet," I said. I knew he was probably sleeping due to a magic spell, but didn't want to scare her. "You just found him like this?" I questioned.

"Yes, I was returning from sending a messenger pigeon about thirty minutes ago and, just as I was coming up the path to the front door, I heard a scream, dashed in, and found the king snoring."

"Do you recognize this?" I asked, holding the coin. The reflection of the flames gave the star a fiery glow.

"Why, I don't think so," he replied nervously.

"I heard the scream from upstairs," volunteered the queen, speaking for the first time. "And I arrived to see Hann standing on the carpet beside the king, crying."

"Did either of you leave this room before I arrived?"

"No," replied the queen. "We stayed here until you came."

"Did you touch anything since you ran in here?" I asked. Hann shook his head.

"No," said the queen with a sob. She cradled her face in her hands. "Will he ever wake?"

Hann patted her back. "I'm sure he will."

"Do you recognize this?" I asked the queen, holding up the coin.

With a sniffle and a wipe of her eyes, she looked up. "I believe we had a guest last week that had a coin like that," she said. "King Joggimir. Do you think he is behind this?"

"I think he might be," interjected Hann the butler.

"I actually have someone else in mind," I answered.

"Who?" demanded the queen.

I pointed to Hann. "Your hired help."

While Hann denied my accusation at first, he eventually broke down and admitted to the crime. He was hoping with Arthur permanently asleep, that the queen would marry him instead. Too bad the queen had no interest.

The queen convinced Hann to give the king the antidote to wake him and it was a success. Hann was to be thrown in the dungeon for his actions against the king, but lucky for him, he was a better runner than a liar—the guards weren't able to catch him when he bolted.

Why did I suspect Hann put the sleeping spell on the king?

HINT: SOMEONE SHOULD COME clean.

SUPER HINT: Don't let this difficult mystery rain on your parade.

The solution is found on page 112

The Case of the Trident Test

SPLASH! I landed in the frigid ocean and instantly inhaled water. The saltiness burned my nose and throat. I swam to shore, sputtering mouthfuls of water, and was relieved when I reached the sandy shore. I took deep inhales of the night air to try to clear my lungs. The full moon reflected on the waveless ocean, and a feeling of calm suddenly washed over me. I didn't know where I was, but it was beautiful.

I was drawn like a moth to the crackling of a fire farther down the shore. A pirate with an eye patch and ratty clothing sat by the warm flames. He wrung out the bottom of his dripping wet shirt as he invited me to join him. I gladly accepted.

The fire felt heavenly against my icy skin, and, within twenty minutes, my clothes were completely dry. I admired the chest of gold under a nearby coconut tree, not daring to ask where my host had gotten it. It was overflowing with pearls, coins, and gems in every color of the rainbow.

"Where are you from?" the pirate finally asked.

"How do you know I'm not from around here?" I asked.

He laughed, showing off a gold tooth. "We don't get many vampires around Pineapple Cove."

My hand flew to my mouth to cover my teeth. *Why didn't the earrings change my teeth?* I wondered. My hands shot up to my earlobes—one of my earrings was missing!

"Don't worry, your secret is safe with me," the pirate said with a wink. I ran to the edge of the water to try to find my lost earring. A mere minute into my search, angry waves lapped at the beach. With a splash larger than a jumping whale, a blue man appeared from the water. His beady eyes pierced the pirate as his flowing blue hair clung to his dewy blue skin.

"You!" the blue man yelled. "You stole my trident." My heart caught in my throat.

The blue man marched toward the pirate.

"I would never do that to you, Poseidon!" said the pirate. "I've been with this girl for the past half hour. She can assure you that." Poseidon turned his attention to me, and I nodded.

"Fine, but my trident went missing an hour ago from my underwater castle. Where were you an hour ago?"

The pirate yawned, as if this sea god's anger bored him. "Sitting around this fire. I haven't budged from this spot in hours."

Poseidon pointed to the treasure chest under the tree. "And where did you steal that bounty from?"

"You think too little of me!" the pirate replied. "I dug it up in the forest. I found it fair and square."

Poseidon's shoulders slumped. "You look like you're telling the truth this time."

"I wouldn't be so sure," I mumbled.

Why did I think the pirate was lying?

HINT: TIMING IS EVERYTHING.

SUPER HINT: This mystery is dripping with clues.

The solution is found on page 113

The Case of the

Enigmatic Egyptian

The air was stale and warm, yet I had a chill shoot through my body. I appeared beside a hooded figure in an Egyptian ruin. Her shadowy eyes were fixated on the statues of painted Egyptians lining the walls. These life-size figures looked like old papier mâché projects with their rough, lumpy finishes and peeling paint. They seemed like they might crumble at any second. Above and below them were painted hieroglyphics on the chipping stone walls. Mostly dancing Egyptians in various poses, but also cats, dogs, and other animals. The trail of dancing Egyptians bordered the entire room. There were two doors, and each dancer above the door was larger than the rest. The one above the left door appeared to be indifferent, shrugging, while the one above the right door appeared to be gleefully doing a jumping jack.

A large crack beside one of the doors caught my eye. As I wandered over, the hooded woman finally spoke.

"The doors are stuck. I've been in here for days and I can't figure out how to open them."

"Maybe you just need a detective to help," I joked. The woman turned to me, pulling back her hood. I recognized her straight black hair and blue eyeliner. It was Cleopatra. But if the Egyptian ruins looked this worn, she was in the wrong time period.

"How did you get here?" I asked.

"I can ask you the same," she answered. "You just appeared out of nowhere."

"Wait, so I'm not a person that was with you the whole time?" I was so confused. In my other time traveling adventures, I simply replaced other detectives, so why was I someone new here? Was the time machine malfunctioning?

Cleopatra sighed. "No, you just appeared seconds ago. I'm here because I sat with a magic woman. She promised me immortality, that I and my people would live forever. Using a lock of my hair, amethyst, and clay, she somehow sent me here." She ran her finger over one of the statues. "But clearly my people don't live forever. And neither shall I if I don't get out of here."

I ran my finger over a crack in the wall, and a black beetle popped out its head. I screamed, stumbling backward onto the golden sarcophagus in the middle of the room.

The room shook, and rocks started crumbling down from the ceiling.

"What have you done?" yelled Cleopatra, dodging a falling rock.

"I don't know!" I said with a shrug.

The left door suddenly opened with a CLUNK.

We rushed to the open door, but the path behind it was caved in with rocks.

"We need to try to open the other door!" Cleopatra cried. "How did you open this one?"

I was so stunned that all I could do was shrug. The left door closed.

How do you open the other door?

HINT: Dᴏɴ'ᴛ ꜱʜʀᴜɢ ᴏꜰꜰ any clues.

SUPER HINT: Imitation is the strongest form of flattery.

The solution is found on page 114

Epilogue

A gust of frigid air propelled me through a dark tunnel, and I reappeared in the time machine.

Lou whipped open the creaky door. "Quick! Get out!" he said. "It's going to blow." We ran to the other side of the room and dove behind a metal table. The machine shook and hollered. The screeching grated at my eardrums, hissing like an angry tea kettle. Then, with a large BANG! and a giant puff of smoke, it stopped. The only sound in the smoky room was Lou and me coughing.

"Is it safe now?" I asked.

Lou cleared his throat. "Only one way to find out." We peeked over the table and squinted at the time machine through the haze. Somehow, it was still in one piece. But that wasn't the most surprising thing—fifteen detectives stood beside it. Some were dressed in distinguished suits and top hats, while others wore togas. A few women wore dresses from various eras.

"Looks like we found those detectives!" Lou said, jumping to his feet. As he explained to the confused bunch how they had gotten there and how he would send them back, I grabbed an apple off a blue plate. Solving fifteen mysteries sure makes you work up an appetite!

After taking out my fake fang so it didn't get stuck in the apple, I dove in. I devoured the juicy fruit as Lou loaded the detectives in the crazy coffin time machine one by one. Soon the detectives were gone and it was just us in the room.

"Phew!" Lou said, wiping his brow. "I'm glad that's over. I can't thank you enough, Hailey. Is there anything I can do to repay you?"

I held up the apple core. "Actually, do you have any more of these apples? Something about this really hit the spot!"

Lou's face turned a sickly white. "Oh no! You didn't eat that apple!? Is that the apple from the blue plate?"

I gulped. "Maybe, why?" Suddenly, my whole body tingled, like when your foot falls asleep. I blinked, and suddenly I was staring at Lou's shoes, on four paws.

"Meow!" I cried.

"Because that apple will turn you into a cat!" Lou said. "But don't worry, I can fix it." He rushed off to dig in a pile of cardboard boxes.

The cozy reading chair in the corner called to me. Deciding there was no point in panicking, I gave in and curled up on the fluffy cushion. It wasn't long before I dozed off—dreaming of my next mystery.

Mystery solving isn't always easy, but it is full of adventures.

Mystery-Solving Tips

Some of these mysteries involve a 'crime' and a 'culprit.' Use the below prompts to take notes as you read and solve each mystery!

Name: Write the name of the suspect, witness, or victim

Motive: Write the reason why a suspect might have committed the 'crime'

Access: Write the time and place it happened

How: Write the way the suspect could have committed the 'crime'

Clues: Write any observations or details that may support the motive, access, or how

Get the Suspect Template at:

scaredybat.com/mm-template

MYSTERIES SOLVED

1. LOST LAPIS LAZULI

WHILE I noticed the blue stain on Caesar's clothing, he wasn't the thief. It was the artist who took the lapis lazuli.

The artist claimed he hadn't had blue paint in weeks, yet mixed purple paint a mere hour ago—a mix of blue and red paint. When I asked him why he stole it, he said he wanted the paintings to be perfect and needed purple for his best work. He didn't think the lapis lazuli would be traced back to him, since he crushed it up to make paint—hiding the evidence.

Luckily, the thief was Cleopatra's favorite artist, so they let him go with a warning. As for Cleopatra's eyeliner, Caesar promised to get her some new lapis lazuli ASAP. I never did find out what the blue stain was on Caesar's clothing, but I suppose not all mysteries need to be solved.

2. SALOON SECRET

IT WOULD have been near impossible for the woman to hastily dial a phone in the dark. Unlike today's cellphones, phones back then didn't have numbers that lit up. I had my suspicions that she couldn't dial in the dark, but just in case my hunch was wrong, I "accidentally" flicked off the lights after I asked her to dial Joseph. Sure enough, she admitted she couldn't dial in the dark.

Turns out she stole the money so she could retire from working at the saloon. She wanted to go on the road and search for gold.

3. DINER DASH

THE FACT that none of the suspect's fingerprints were on the dishes or silverware used while eating convicted him. In wiping his own prints from the items he handled, he destroyed all prints—those of the waitress, cook, etc. After I made the solve, I was able to get a plate of fries before time traveling to my next mystery. And I must say, he should have just stuck to his meal. It was delicious! And I doubt they serve fries in jail.

4. GLADIATOR GAMBIT

THE GUARD automatically grabbed the other fighters' wands. Yet, the guard never even reached for Promegon's. If Promegon really didn't know anyone there, how would the guard have known that Promegon didn't allow anyone to touch his wand before battle? After all, the referee had a hard time finding anything about Promegon.

Therefore, it is reasonable to assume the guard and Promegon had met before. Eventually Promegon admitted to the crime. The two men were going to sell the wand to get gold to flee Rome—turns out this wasn't their first heist.

5. ROYAL RUSE

I SUSPECT the queen. She claims that she had new shoes and hadn't left the room she was in since early the day before. Yet, they were muddy.

I later found out that she had to run to the castle gate in order to get the poison after her new shoes arrived. Hence, why they were muddy. She handed off the poison to a server who spiked Henry's drink while no one was looking. Unluckily for Eleanor, Henry made a full recovery.

Soon after, Eleanor's sons revolted against King Henry. The revolt failed and Eleanor was captured and semi-imprisoned in England. Her imprisonment came to an end when Henry died from an ulcer in 1189.

6. CAVE CONUNDRUM

THE RABBITS were the treasure! You had to continue looking at the rabbits on the other walls and move through the doors backwards to get through. Rabbits were considered very important to this tribe, which is why they were the only wall drawings in gold. This door was so hard to get through because many people assumed that you had to stare at the gems on the door.

7. POTION PROBLEM

A RAINBOW orb shattered falling off the second shelf in the supply closet. If the four-tier shelf in the office was shoved to the ground as the woman stated, the glass orbs on the top shelf would have surely shattered.

The woman eventually admitted to stealing the dragon's breath for a wizard that was offering a rare cloak in return. However, she couldn't bear to break the rainbow glass orbs, so she removed them before tipping the shelf and then placed them on the floor.

8. SALEM SCANDAL

I WAS suspicious of John, the nephew. Upon being asked where he was at the time of the robbery, he stated he was "hauling in a muskie." Unless he stole the jewels, he couldn't possibly have known at what time the robbery was committed.

Sure enough, John did it. Worried his aunt would get Amira exiled for being a witch, he stole the gold to run off with Amira and start a life together. Gold was rare back then, so it was worth a lot. The gardener was burying a necklace that John had sent him out to fetch. John returned the gold and, with only a necklace and some fish to his name, left with Amira that night.

Amira escaped the possibility of being accused and prosecuted during the Salem Witch Trials. Between February 1692 and May 1693, more than 200 people were accused of being witches in Salem.

9. PETRIFIED PASSENGER

With Jeffrey's topcoat buttoned, there would have been no way for the glass from his pocket watch to scatter everywhere when he fell facedown. It was later found that the girl in the yellow dress cast the spell after Jeffrey caught her trying to rob him. The watch broke in the fight, and she placed it back in his pocket before rolling him facedown. A doctor onboard was able to unfreeze Jeffrey, but the ship sank a few days later.

10. BLUEPRINT BURGLARY

In such a small room, the intruder would *unquestionably* have heard Percy aka the shapeshifting elf dialing headquarters. There was no way they could be unaware of his presence.

The elf was sent by someone that Percy refused to sell the blueprints to. His job was to pull a heist on the buyer, but he couldn't find them. He shapeshifted into Percy and called in hoping that the detective would lead him to the secret buyer. But his story was flawed and he didn't get very far. The real Percy was found unharmed in the basement.

11. REPTILE RIDDLE

THE TOWER of glasses still being upright is fishy. Had Tom fallen on the table after he transformed back into a human, the table shake would have knocked over the "crazily balanced glasses." As the detective found the glasses on the table, *balanced*, it was obvious Tom had been carefully placed on the table after he passed out. Why, you ask? That part we may never know!

12. INHERITANCE INTRIGUE

THE MAN didn't have a brother, but he did have a sister—the gender of the producer was never stated. His sister, the producer, got the inheritance.

13. CAMELOT CURSE

HAD HANN dashed into the entrance like he said he did, there would have been muddy foot tracks in the entrance. Remember, to get in, the knights "led me through mud and rain" to the front door and found the entrance spotless. Even if he had cleaned, if he had been standing on the white rug as the queen claimed, he wouldn't have had time to scrub out those mud stains. Therefore, Hann was lying, which made him a prime suspect.

14. TRIDENT TEST

IF THE pirate had really been hanging around the fire "for hours," then his clothes wouldn't have still been dripping when I first met him. My sopping wet clothes only took twenty minutes to dry around the fire. While I didn't rat the pirate out to Poseidon, he figured it out, and the pirate gave him back the trident. As for my earring, it seems to be lost at sea forever. Maybe it will be someone else's treasure one day.

15. ENIGMATIC EGYPTIAN

THE DOORS open and close when the dance move painted above them is imitated. Shrugging opened and closed the left door, which meant that jumping jacks opened the right one.

Cleopatra and I were able to figure it out and escape before the ruins crumbled. Before I could ask her more questions about her time travel, she disappeared in a cloud of dust. I guess not all mysteries are meant to be solved.

WHAT'S NEXT

Did you enjoy these History Mysteries?

Then you'll love the other Hailey Haddie Minute Mystery books!

Continue the mystery-solving fun by visiting

scaredybat.com/minutemysteries

Already read the other Minute Mysteries?

Coming Soon: Hailey Haddie's Minute Mysteries Egypt Edition

Uh oh! Hailey and Lou accidentally changed history during their last time travel adventure. And now the pyramids in Egypt are disappearing. Join Hailey as she solves the mystery!

Be first to know when it's released:
Visit scaredybat.com/mm-egypt

Discussion Questions

(1) What did you enjoy about these minute mystery stories?

(2) Which story was your favorite?

(3) What are some of the story themes?

(4) Were you able to solve the mysteries? How did you do it?

(5) Detective Superpowers: Would you rather speak any language or change your appearance to blend in with any environment?

(6) What other books, shows, or movies do these stories remind you of?

(7) If you could talk to the author, what is one question you would ask her?

DEAR READER,

Hello there! Did you enjoy these short mystery stories? I know I did!

If you want to join the team as we solve more mysteries, then leave a review!

Otherwise, we won't know if you're up for the next case. And when we go to solve it, you may never hear about it!

You can leave a review wher-ever you found the book.

I'm excited to see you for the next mystery adventure!

Fingers crossed it's a super interesting one...

Yours Truly,

Detective Hailey Haddie

Also By Marina J. Bowman

SCAREDY BAT
A fear-busting vampire detective series
#1 Scaredy Bat and the Frozen Vampires
#2 Scaredy Bat and the Sunscreen Snatcher
#3 Scaredy Bat and the Missing Jellyfish
#4 Scaredy Bat and the Haunted Movie Set
#5 Scaredy Bat and the Mega Park Mystery
#6 Scaredy Bat and the Art Thief
#7 Scaredy Bat and the Dragon Necklace

HAILEY HADDIE MINUTE MYSTERIES
Solve-them-yourself supernatural mysteries

MISFIT MAGIC SCHOOL
Ember failed her magic exam...Now what?

THE LEGEND OF PINEAPPLE COVE
A mythical sea-faring adventure series

About the Author

MARINA J. BOWMAN is a writer and explorer who travels the world searching for wildly fantastical stories to share with her readers.

Marina enjoys sailing, flying, and nearly all other forms of transportation. She stays away from the spotlight to maintain privacy and ensure the more unpleasant secrets she uncovers don't catch up with her.

As a matter of survival, Marina nearly always communicates with the public through her representative, Devin Cowick, founder of Code Pineapple books.

24166614R00076